Quest for Success

Making Money through Service

Quest for Success

Making Money Through Service

Marsha Ferrick Heiden, PhD., BCC

Author

Marie Billings Dalton

Artist

Quest for Success

Making Money through Service

Written by Marsha Ferrick Heiden, PhD., BCC

Cover by Marie Billings Dalton

Copyright 2016

Marsha Ferrick Heiden, PhD, BCC
Amara Quest, Inc.
8322 State Route 305
Garrettsville, OH 44231

http://www.amaraquest.com

In Memory of:

John A. Ritola

Dedicated to:

Nancy

Seeker's Name

```
┌────────────────────────────────────┐
│                                    │
│                                    │
└────────────────────────────────────┘
```

Date

Table of Contents

vi

Quest for Success

Quests are journeys that are a search for something. To begin a business that is a service is a specific type of Quest. Success comes from designing, and delivering a service that will benefit others by adding value to their lives, and yours. Quests are full of challenges, or as I like to think of them creative opportunities. *The Holy Grail* is the summary of your Quest and will be completed at the end of this guide.

The real value of planning is the creative process you undertake as you consider your business in a meaningful way. The process of planning helps you to think things through thoroughly, study, research, and look at your ideas creatively and critically. Although it takes time a well thought out business helps avoid some problems along the way.

The planning of a business varies greatly depending on what you ultimately seek. The most important thing to do if you are in earnest about your business is to set aside time in your daily calendar to prepare, plan, and carry out your business. Failure to set aside time is the greatest obstacle to beginning your business. So if you wish to be one of those people who can say at the end of their life you have no regrets then block time on your calendar and make creating your business a priority in your life.

Your Quest

Describe the quest you want to take. What is your mission? In less than thirty words explain your main reason for creating this business. Your mission will be the basis of all the important decisions you will make. Place this mission statement where you can see it every day.

The Treasure

What do you want to master[1]? You will need to master running a business. You can be great at what you do but without mastering the art of creating a successful business your talent and service may go to waste. How do you define success? What goals do you have for your business? Be specific. Where do you want to end up when your business is up and running? For example, you might have a goal to have a healthy, successful business that focuses on customer service with a high referral rate and loyal customer following. If it would be helpful create a vision board. Be specific, and illustrate your goal with words, drawings, pictures, or photos for inspiration. It is helpful to have specific measurable goals for defining success so that you can celebrate each one as you reach it.

---

[1] Recommended reading: *Mastery: The Keys to Success and Long-Term Fulfillment.* George Leonard (1992)

What are the stepping stones to each of your goal(s)? Create progress markers along the journey to achieve your goals. For example, a stepping stone might be a specific quarterly sales marker and some specific measures of your customers' satisfaction. Be specific, and illustrate your goal with words, drawings, pictures, or photos for inspiration. Make the goals realistic and as you complete each step place a new visual reminder of your current "next step." Make it doable. Small baby steps are better than large leaps. That doesn't mean there are not times you will make a big leap just remember it is your day to day grit that keeps you consistently moving toward your next goal.

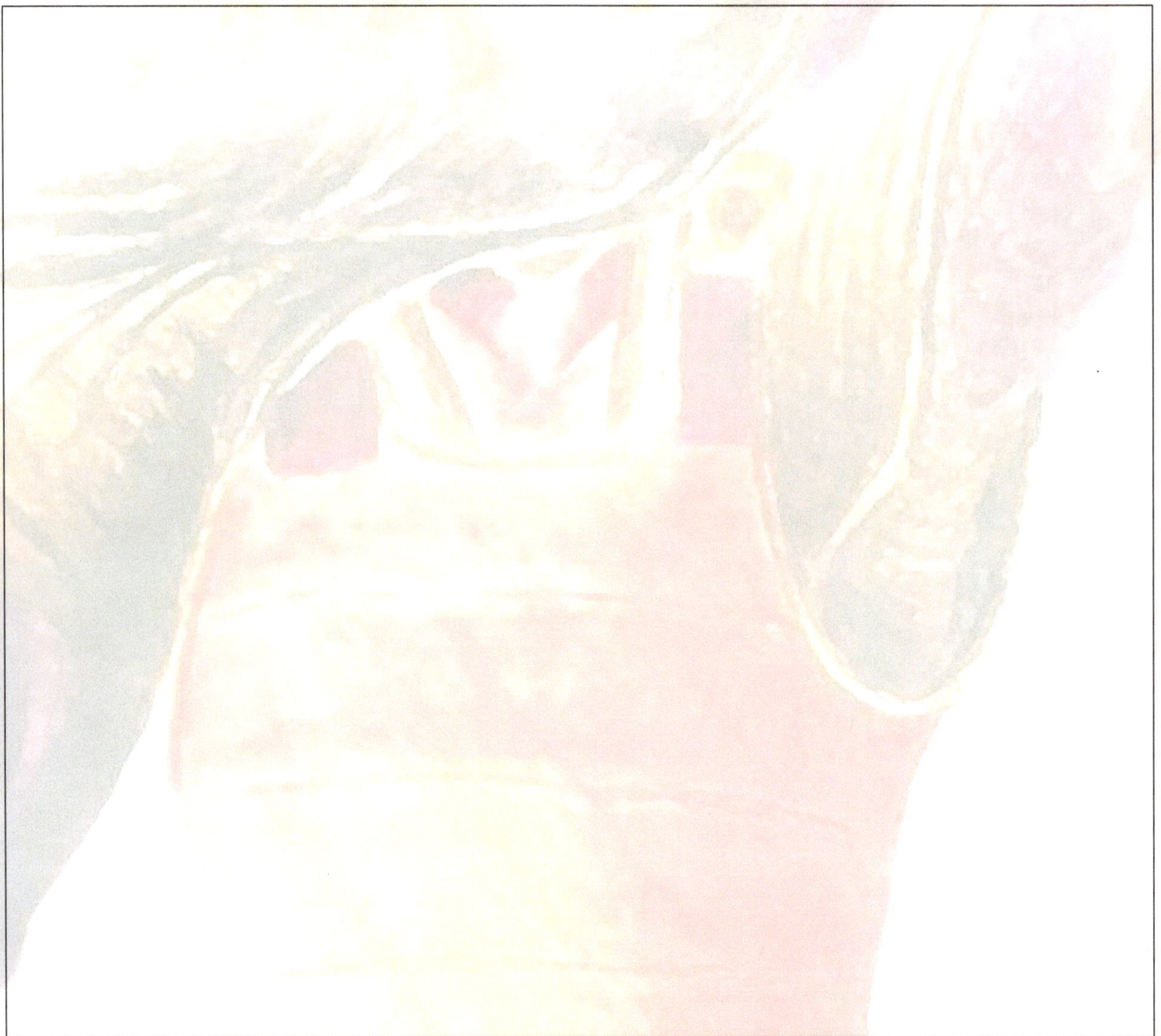

Quest Philosophy

My philosophy of life is that if we make up our mind what we are going to make of our lives,
then work hard toward that goal, we never lose - somehow we win out.
Ronald Reagan

What is important to you about your business?

Whom will your business impact? This might relate to who you will be
impacted by your services consider clients, employees, you, and your family.

How will your business impact your clients?

How will it impact your employees?

What changes do you foresee in your life because of your business? Short-term? Long-term?

How will your business impact you and your family?

Keep it simple without sacrificing quality or value.

Operating a business efficiently is paramount to success. Keep your operating process as simple and sleek as possible. Creating complex systems and processes costs money to develop, start, and maintain. So practice the KISS principle, Keep It Simple Sweetheart! What systems will you need? How will each of these systems operate? Be as specific and detailed as possible while keeping it simple and straightforward. In this case less is more. Less stuff is more money for you, your family, your employees, and more value for your clients.

Start with what you want to create. Consider the ultimate result that you want to achieve then work backward until you know where to start? To begin, start with baby steps. Start close to home and build your business outward without getting drawn into the lure of expensive marketing options that are out there that can drain your money. Start with one prospect and serve one prospect at a time. Likewise create effective systems as you need them. Effective systems are those that create the outcomes that you want. So if you don't like the results then evaluate your system. Where does your system need to be adjusted or changed?

Daily Operations

How will those you serve obtain your services?

What will be your hours? How many of those will be allocated to serving prospects or current clients? How many will be allocated for other business issues? Consider that scarcity increases value. What days of the week, and weeks of the year will you take off? How many days per week will you work?

How will you manage clients that do not follow through? Do not return calls or do not show up?

Location

Where will your daily operations be located? Consider the flow of your business. How will you best serve your people logistically? This will vary greatly depending upon the nature of your services. Some services may not require that you have a physical space to meet your client while other types of services may require it.

Do you need a precise location? Can you operate out of your home? What needs will your physical location have to fulfill for your business? Consider the amount of space, type of building, zoning, power and other utilities needed for your business. Consider access for your clients. Is your location important to those you serve? If yes, how? Is it convenient? Parking? Interior spaces? Not out of the way? Is it consistent with your image? Is it what prospects want and expect? Is it important that your location be convenient to transportation or other agencies or conveniences? Do you need easy walk-in access? What are your requirements for parking and proximity to freeway, airports, or local transportation? Most new businesses should not sink capital into construction, but if you are planning to build, costs and specifications will be a big part of your plan. Estimate the expenses of occupying your space, including rent, if you do not own the space. Don't forget to include maintenance, utilities, insurance, and initial remodeling costs to make the space suit your needs. These numbers are part of your financial plan.

Environment

What type of environment do you want to work in? How will you create that environment for yourself, your employees, prospects, and clients? Why will this environment serve you, your employees, prospects and clients?

Human Resources

Will you need employees or contractors to operate your business? If so, what employees will you need as sojourners with you in your business? What will be your hiring and letting go process? Who will you need with you on your quest? What type of employees will you need, skilled, unskilled, and/or professional? Where and how will you find the right sojourners? What will be your pay structure? How will you train your sojourners? Who will do which tasks? What schedules and written procedures will need to be prepared? Draft job descriptions for each sojourner. Will you use contract workers or employees?

Equipment & Supplies

What equipment will you need to run your business efficiently? What are the costs? What quality will you need? Where will you purchase it? What supplies will you need to replenish? Where will you purchase your supplies? Identify key suppliers list their names and contact information. Why have you chosen these specific suppliers?

Legal Issues

What legal form of ownership will your business become: sole proprietor, partnership, corporation, limited liability corporation (LLC)?   Why have you selected this form?

What are the legalities of your business? Consider licensing and bonding requirements, permits, health, workplace, or environmental regulations, special regulations covering your industry or profession, zoning or building code requirements, insurance coverage, trademarks, copyrights, or patents (pending, existing, or purchased). Which if any of these apply to your business? Consult with an attorney if you are in doubt about any legal requirements that you might need to consider for your business.

Trading

What are your payment policies? Do you plan to sell on credit? Do you really need to sell on credit? Does it serve you or your clients to sell on credit? Is it customary in your industry and expected by your clientele? If yes, what policies will you have about who gets credit and how much? How will you check the creditworthiness of new applicants? What terms will you offer your customers; that is, how much credit and when is payment due? Will you offer prompt payment discounts? Do this only if it is usual and customary in your industry. Do you know what it will cost you to extend credit? Have you built the costs into your prices? What are the pricing, or fees for your services?

Organization

How will you manage and organize your business? Who will manage your business on a day-to-day basis? If that person is not you then what experience does the person you hire need to bring to your business? What special or distinctive competencies? Is there a plan for continuation of your business if this person is lost or incapacitated? Create a chart showing the hierarchy and who is responsible for what on your journey. Include position descriptions and resumes for key sojourners. Who will you rely on for advice on your business? Consider the following: A coach to assist you in overseeing your business. You may desire directors to help you oversee the big picture of your company. Who will advise your employees? From whom will you seek advice and assistance for legal, financial, and insurance risk matters? Will you need specific advice and assistance in other areas of your business? If so from whom? How can you keep your life, and business clean and simple? How can you avoid busyness and focus on money producing tasks?

Competitive Advantage

What factors give you a competitive advantages or disadvantages? Examples include level of quality, service, or unique expertise. Describe your business from the point of view of those it will be serve. How is your business going to be crazy good? How are you going to go above and beyond to serve your customers? Describe how this will benefit your clients? Consider the features (concrete facts of your business) and benefits (what will be gained by clients) of your business. What are they? What ongoing services will be provided? How will you discuss the logistics? The investment, the procedure? How will you know the prospect is really invested? Write down stories that illustrate each of the features and benefits your services provides to customers.

The Map

All you need is the plan, the road map, and the courage to press on to your destination.
Earl Nightingale

The first challenge of any quest is to create a map. A map of where you want to go and how you will get there from where you are now. A successful business has to create maps or systems for these areas: factors of Influence, value, high levels of compensation, your authenticity in the form of self-knowledge, effective momentum, and leadership, and receptivity[2] to help you get from where you are now to where you want your business to be.

The creation of these map should not be set down in pen but with pencil because you will make many changes, and adjustments to this guide. You will want to always evaluate your map, and where you are at and what needs to be tweaked in order to stay on course in each area in order to meet your goals.

Where are you now?

```



```

Where do you want to be?

```



```

---

[2] Recommended reading, *The Go-Giver* by Bob Burg and John David Mann (2015)

The Challenge of Influence

Your influence is determined by how abundantly you place other people's interest first.[3]

Are you a part of the *"Ego Era"* or the *"Generosity Generation?"* Michael J Maher in *The Seven Levels of Communication*[4]: *Go from Relationships to Referrals* referred to businesses in previous decades as "The Ego Era." *"This was a period of time where personal promotion, self-absorption, and image advertising were rampant. It was all about the business owner. It was about the me. All about me. These businesses fed the ego."* Maher goes on to refer to the current business environment as the *"Generosity Generation."* *"The Generosity Generation is the business era where generous acts are rewarded. Givers are uniting to make a difference in the world. It is about the consumer. It is about the "you". It is all about relationships. These businesses feed the soul."* This quest is yours to feed your soul.

Get the Word Out

Who needs to know about your business and why? No matter your business it will be necessary for people to know that your business exists. Consider who needs to know? Some business will require only a few people know. Begin with careful consideration and possibly research[5].

---

[3] *The Go-Giver* by Bob Burg and John David Mann (2015)

[4] Recommended reading *The Seven Levels of Communication: Go from Relationships to Referrals* by Michael J. Mahler (2014)

[5] There are two kinds of research that is done in preparation for a Quest, primary and secondary. Secondary research uses published information that is available on-line, in libraries, and from other public sources of information. Remember that not all sources are

List your support system. The consider who else will need to know to make your business a success?

```



```

How to Tell

How will you tell them? How will you get the word out to those that need to know? How will you get the word out to those you want to serve on your quest? Consider starting with your inner circle. Then talking to and inviting one person at a time to experience your service, if they are interested.

```



```

created equal so evaluate who has completed the research that you use and the quality of the study. Research librarians can be especially helpful. Primary research is data that you have gathered on your own. Some examples would be a traffic count at a proposed location, use of the yellow pages to identify competitors, and surveys or focus-group interviews to learn about consumer preferences. As you consider your Quest, be as specific as possible; give statistics, numbers, and sources. The plan you are developing will be the basis of the important decision you will make on your Quest.

Go Pro

To succeed at your business, you will need to become an expert and a professional. How will you attain this status in your own eyes, as well as the eyes of those you serve? What image do you want to project? How do you want to be seen? How will you ensure that happens? How will you reinvent[6] yourself?

Consider that serving is not pleasing but kindly assisting your clients for their best interest. How will you do that without falling into "people pleasing mode"?

---

[6] Recommended reading, *Reinventing Yourself: How to Become the Person You've Always Wanted to Be* (2005) by Steve Chandler.

Their World

Remember that enrollments and sales take place in your prospect's world not yours so get into their world. Keep your focus there. Build your business one prospect at a time. This may be your business but the outcome will depend on how well you live in the land and world of your prospective clients. So first consider what they want? What do they want to change? Be interested in them. How do you help prospective clients feel relaxed and safe so they will want to continue talking with you? Learn about your prospects and their wants. Wait until they ask you about your services. Use stories about current or previous clients to illustrate how your services can assist them.

Client Acquisition

How can you set your business up so that a prospect's only decision is to continue to work with you, not whether to start with you or not? How will you know if you are on the right track with this process? How will you arrange for uninterrupted time to talk with prospects? How will you follow-up with prospective clients?

Problem Solving

Be a problem solver, but first be a great listener. How can you solve your prospects problems? Sustain focus on their problems. How can you help them brings those problems to resolution?

How might you use humor to create great relationships with your prospects? How might you resolve business relationship issues by using techniques you use to resolve issues with your friends and family members?

Elevate Them

How can you intentionally meet your prospects in a way that elevates them? How can you make a difference in their life? Get to know about your prospects, be curious, and investigate. What did you find out? What questions will you ask them?

It's All about Serving

Service is a making a profound difference in people's lives through an exchange of money. True service can only be provided through an exchange of money or something of value, otherwise people will not show up fully. Love what you do, and do it because you love it not because you need the money or the sale.

Obtaining clients occurs first through connection and then through service. How will you reach out and connect with your prospects? How can you make that connection meaningful? How can you slow things down? Develop the relationship? Instead of thinking about *"How can I sell them?"* think *"How can I help them right away?"* How can you make talking to you and investing in your service be something they love to do, and want to continue doing? How can you raise your listening and service to that type of level? How can you insure that your prospect gets something from your time together? How can you help this prospect? How can you use your enthusiasm to support your prospect? How will you look for problems that you can help prospects solve with your services? How can you help your prospective clients get past their hidden fears of working with you? How do you assure them that they cannot fail as one of your clients?

Obstacles

Consider what obstacles that your prospects might be facing. How can you address those obstacles such as a spouse, boss, or someone else that might be influencing your prospect?

The Importance of Money

Remember that you always serve best when there is an exchange of money. Money is energy. Money impacts the way people show up for an experience. Do your customers a favor charge for your services so they will show up and use your services effectively. People value what they invest in. How will you make sure your clients value your services? Remember if people say they cannot afford your services don't take it personally. It doesn't mean your prices are too high it means they do not see the value in it for themselves. Those same folks will take the 16 grandchildren to Disneyland next month. Their finances are none of your business. Move on to the next person.

Create an Experience

Potential clients are more likely to purchase your service if they can have an experience of you and/or your service. How can you create an experiential situation for your prospects to create an experience of you and your services? How can you make it easy for your prospect to work with you? How will you assist people in utilizing your services? How will you create referral sources with an experience of you and/or an experiential understanding of your services?

Challenging

What benefits might you find in challenging your prospects "yes" to work with you? How might trying to talk people out of your service be helpful? How might you do that? When would it be beneficial to have this type of conversation? Consider using this when the prospect is ambivalent about investing in your services. Why might that be effective?

Be in Charge

How can you improve your conversations with prospective clients? How can you continue contact with prospects and clients without selling? What will your process be? How will you lead the conversations? How will you be in charge of the next contact time? How can you express your curiosity in a person that may not necessarily be seeking your services? How can you express your curiosity in person that you know is seeking your services? How would those conversations differ?

Referrals

When you do get a referral? How will you slow down and listen openly to your newly-referred prospect? How will you follow up with your referral source?

Share the Love

How can more time and more love be beneficial to your business? How can you act from a place of love in your business? Why is this important? How will this impact your clients?

Where to Start?

Who do you know? With whom will you start? Start with those you know. Start with who you already know? How can you serve them? How will you ask?

Make a list of all the people you would like to serve. Who would you love to serve? How could you meet them? How could you help them? How can you learn more about them? How can you create relationships? How can you jump in and have fun meeting people? How are you willing to risk to develop relationships?

Drawing In

Listening is always a great way to draw others to you, it is better than talking. How can you continue to improve your listening? How can you learn to listen without judgment? How can you be an engaged listener? How can you learn to listen to the meaning behind the words? Be specific. How can you slow down? Slow down and stay in the conversation with your prospects. How can you challenge and encourage your prospects to work with you? What stories can you tell them of successes you have had with other client that have similar experiences to theirs? Don't forget to return the conversation to the prospect's world?

Creating Community

How can you create a community? How will you stay connected with prospects and clients? How can you grow a network and help others to grow theirs? Connecting with others can be simplified by keeping the idea of helping whoever you meet. Google those you meet to learn more about them. Be punctual or early to any events or appointments that you schedule. Introduce yourself and be interested in the other. Remember the word FROG[7] to help in building rapport. Ask about Family, Recreation, Occupation, and Goals then follow up. Get people on your schedule, and send a follow-up note.

---

[7] M.J.Mahler (2014) The Seven Levels of Communication: Go from Relationships to Referrals

Ideas for Creating Prospects

Check the ones that might work for you:

— Send emails inquiring about the well-being of your prospects.

— Becoming a regular at a local restaurant to create an office away from the office.

— Develop some great question such as, "How can I help you?" or "What can I do for you?"

— Use body language that matching or mirroring your prospects. Align your movement and pattern of speech with the other person. If there excited be excited. If they are subdued be subdued. In a one-on-one meeting mirroring the physical actions of the other person. Don't overdo it but enough so that others feel connected to you. You can also repeat an affirmation back to the affirming person using the second person (You). Phrases like "tell me more about that" and "what is important about that to you" allows you to find the underlying motivations for your prospects.

— If you enjoy writing then create personal, optimistic, hand written notes that are effective and relational that build trust and get responses. Use the word "You" as much as possible and avoid words "I, My, Me, and We" (except in terms of you and the person you are writing). Be specific with praise. Use the power of positive projection. Write correctly. Be interested in their world.

— Being introduced through a mutual friend builds trust rapidly. If my friend trusts you, I am more likely to trust you. Trust can be borrowed then built upon. You can create a business quickly and profitably through introduction of mutual friends.

— Join a local organization.

— Attend groups where your prospects might go.

— Attend to FB and LI social media. Look for people that would benefit from your services then reach out, connect, invite them to an experience of your service, if the prospect is interested after the experience then discuss the logistics of working with you.

— Invite people to events that you sponsor or put on.

— Speak for local audiences.

— Blogs or posts.

— Read your emails. Someone might need your services. Be open to opportunities to serve people in all types of settings.

In what other ways will you create prospects for your business? Start with one at a time.

The Challenge of Compensation

Your income is determined by how many people you serve and how well you serve them.[8]

The Generosity Generation[9] achieves wealth through service. The Challenge of Compensation is to determine methods of serving greater numbers. Most of the time having the lowest price is not a good policy. It robs you of a needed profit margin which you will need to serve in greater ways. Price is only one thing that people consider when they purchase a product or service. You can always be underpriced by competitors. Usually you will do better to have average or above average investment options for those you serve and provide quality and outstanding services. There are a number of costs you will need to consider when considering your price. Remember the more someone invests with you the more committed they are to your services.

Services

List your services.

---

[8] *The Go-Giver* by Bob Burg and John David Mann (2015)

[9] M.J.Mahler (2014) The Seven Levels of Communication: Go from Relationships to Referrals

Credit Policy

What are your credit policies? And costs? If you will be taking credit cards, consider the costs involved and add that to your cost column. Taking credit is a personal decision and there are pros and cons to using credit options. What are the pluses of taking credit cards such as the ability to serve greater numbers, and get paid up front? Then consider the cons including the extra cost of using credit or credit cards. What are the cons?

Pros	Cons

Financial Management

The first rule of thumb in starting a business is keep it simple and fun[10]. Consider the expenses you may have before you even begin operating your business. Estimate these expenses as accurately as you can, then plan for sufficient funds for these expenses. Research your expenses and estimate them carefully. Always add a special contingency category for unexpected expenses that might arise. Talk to others who have started similar businesses to get a good idea of how much to allow for contingencies. If you cannot get good information, a rule of thumb is to use at least 20 percent of the total of all other start-up expenses for contingencies. Make note of how you decided upon your projected expenses. Your sources may be important, as you continue with financing your business.

It is helpful to have a financial plan that consists of a 12-month profit and loss projection, a four-year profit and loss projection (optional), a cash-flow projection, a projected balance sheet, and a break-even calculation. This

---

[10] Recommended reading: *100 Ways to Create Wealth: 9 Lies that are Holding Your Business Back,* Steve Chandler and Sam Beckford (2007).

plan is a reasonable estimate of your business's financial future and will provide you with insight on how to proceed with your business.

The point of developing a financial plan is to determine how much you need before startup, for preliminary expenses, operating expenses, and reserves. You will need to keep it updated as you move forward. It will enable you to foresee anticipate and plan for times of plenty and seasons of leanness. If you do not have experience with financial plans consider hiring a certified financial planner, or certified public accountant to assist you with this important part of your business.

How will you complete your financial plans? Will you complete them on your own? If you will not, who will you hire and how will you know they are competent to do the work you need?

Do you have an accountant? If not I highly recommend that you hire one or at the very least consult with one regarding your initial start-up and operational costs, along with how to manage taxes, payroll, and cash flow. Who will manage your finances?

Start-up Costs

Non-recurring costs associated with setting up a business, such as accountant's fees, legal fees, registration charges, as well as advertising, promotional activities, and employee training are referred to as start-up costs. Also referred to as startup expenses, preliminary expenses, or pre-opening expenses. What will it cost to get started on your Quest? What will your initial start-up costs be?

Capital Costs

Capital costs are fixed, one-time expenses incurred on the purchase of land, buildings, construction, and equipment used in the production of goods or in the rendering of services. Put simply, it is the total cost needed to bring a project to an operational status.[11] What capital costs will you have, if any for your business?

---

[11] Wikipedia

Operational Fixed Costs

Operational fixed costs are items such as rent, that are constant whatever the amount of services you produce each month.[12] What will your operational fixed costs be? What will it cost to run your business on a month to month basis? What will it cost to sell you services?

Operational Variable Costs

Operational variable costs vary with the level of your output.[13] For each unit of service, you create what does that additional cost you? Variable costs do not occur when you are not producing a unit of service. For example, if you pay rent by the month then rent is a fixed cost but if you pay rent only for the time you are seeing a client in that room then it becomes a variable cost. What will the cost of one unit of service sold cost you?

[12] Google

[13] Google

Break-Even Point

The break-even point is the point at which cost or expenses and revenue are equal.[14] Given your operational and variable costs. How much income will you need to break even each month? Break-even calculators are available online.

Pay Yourself

Do not forget to pay yourself. How much will you need to live on?

Asset Assessment

Financing your business may be challenging. So list your personal assets, liabilities, and personal net worth. You may have to draw on personal assets to finance your business, and these statements will show you what is available.

[14] Wikipedia

Pricing

How will you determine your prices? Author and coach Steve Chandler suggests that you not set a fair price but consider what a fun price for your products or services might be. Place your hand on your heart. Say your fun price aloud to yourself, then say a lesser price. Now say a price higher than your fun price. What feels right in your heart and body? Remember you want your prospects to be committed to your service, and money creates a commitment. What did you determine from this exercise? If in doubt start at the lower price. It is easier to raise prices, and you do not want to discount your services.

Payment

How will you get paid? How about upfront? What will be your procedure for ensuring payment?

Raising Prices

When will you raise your prices? Remember your time is limited and that increases your value. How will that impact your pricing and decisions? How will you know it is time to raise your prices? Be concrete.

Family and Friend Rates

What rates will you charge your friends and family for your services? I suggest you consider not discounting your services and definitely do not give them away for free. The value they will receive from it will be directly proportional to the investment that they make in your services. Serve them well by charging them.

Financial Independence Plan

What is your plan with money[15]? How can you create a system that helps you relax and build your wealth? Consider the following types of accounts such as a Rainy Day Fund (3-6 months of expenses in case of an emergency), Retirement, Savings, Business Expenses, Taxes, Your Salary. Be specific about your needs.

[15] Recommended reading: *Overcoming Under Earning: A Five Step Plan to a Richer Life,* Barbara Stanny (2005)

The Challenge of Value

True worth is determined by giving more in value then you take in payment.[16]

How will you use truth telling as a way to add value to your service? After having a conversation with a potential client consider ways in which you can be helpful to them. Send them a gift, a video clip, a quote, card, or message. Make a list of possible ways you could serve a prospect without selling them something. How can you blow away your prospects? How can you create enough value up front? How can you make it feel crazy for them to go without you? How can you put in more heart and love right from the beginning to for your clients?

[16] *The Go-Giver* by Bob Burg and John David Mann (2015)

The Beneficiaries

Identify those that you want to work with and that will benefit from your business. What are their characteristics? Geographic locations? What are their demographics? You may have different groups of people that will benefit from your business make sure to identify each group and determine a demographic profile for each group: age, gender, location, income level, social class, occupation, and education. What other factors might be important to consider? Remember you want to create a business of clients that *you love* working with on a regular business.

Blockades

Who and what will get in your way of creating your business?

[ ]

Yourself

How will you get in your own way? How will you keep from meeting your goals? How will you prevent this from occurring?

[ ]

Others

Who will get in your way? Who will keep you from meeting your goals? List them. How will they get in your way? How will you prevent them?

[ ]

Benefits

How will you create differences that will benefit your prospects? What makes your business special? Where do you fit in the world? Systematically analyzed your environment to obtain a clear picture of where your business fits into the world. In one short paragraph, define your unique business.

Relationships

How will you love your clients? How will you surprise your clients? What can you do that is unexpected? How can you use random acts to strengthen your relationships? How will your clients know you appreciate them? How will you express your appreciation to them? How will you make your clients as grateful as you are for their business? How will you give them more than they give you? How can use love instead of fear to bring people to you? How can you give without expectation and receive joy in return? How can you create prospect astonishment? How can you give to others? Consider that giving will increase your abundance? Give thoughtful gifts from the spirit? Consider using Google Alerts to find useful items on Google that relate to your client. Stay solution focused for your clients. Why will people come to you and pay for your services?

Solutions

List of solutions provided by your business. What are your success stories?
How will you relate these stories to prospects?

Success Story

How can you create conversations with people? How can use language that invites people to stay in relationship with you? Keep things simple. What do you love to do? How can that be the basis of creating clients or customers? What stories can you tell about the features and benefits of your services? Write these stories out. Practice telling them. Help people create pictures in their minds. Pictures are active in the right side of our brain where we feel emotions and get excited. What will make them say "I want that for me?" Write out your success stories. What was the situation? What would have been the worst case scenario if you weren't involved? How did you help your client solve the problem? What was the result? Be specific. What did the prospect say or do to let you know you did well?

The Challenge of Authenticity

The most valuable gift you have to offer is yourself.[17]

How can you create actions from your genuine concerns? How can you bring your happiness with you when you deal with your potential clients? How can you use personal vulnerability to appropriately open up your clients? Appropriately revealing yourself improves your relationships with others. How can you appropriately reveal yourself in your relationships? How can your prospects experience you? Prospects can experience you in many ways. You can be experienced in person via face to face meetings, phone calls, or via media video, audio, or through writing such as books, emails, articles, blog or on-line posts. Certainly the preference is for prospects to meet you face to face, however phone calls, emails, and texts as well as other media can be effective means for your prospects to gain an experience of you.

---

[17] *The Go-Giver* by Bob Burg and John David Mann (2015)

51

Effective Momentum

Everything is created in action. How will you keep going? When you have a successful call or sale, DON'T STOP! How will you continue to be the best in your business? Consider the system you will use to create momentum. What will it look like? How can you remain in action? What will assist you in always bringing your best to your clients?

Creating Space

Consider the journey you are about to embark on. Do you have time and room in your life your business? Given your current environment can you meet your goals? Can you serve effectively given your current circumstances? Is there room to increase your ability to serve others?

Obstacle Overcoming

What obstacles are you facing? How will you overcome these obstacles to create room for your business?

Energy Enhancers vs Energy Drainers

Determine which activities produce income and those that do not. What are energy sucking activities with little or no income production? Look at your calendar where are you spending most of your time? Increase the time you spend in activities that lead to making money. Most of the time that will mean spending your time in conversations that are money talks not social talks. These type of discussions are spent in the other person's world where sales are made. How are you not attending to the issues that increase income?

Energy & Income Enhancers

Energy & Income Drainers

Reach Out, Connect, Invite, Create, Propose

What system will you develop so that you know who your next conversation will be with each day? One conversation at a time. How will you reach out, connect or reconnect, invite, create an experience for them, and then propose that they work with you? Take your time slow down.

Errors

Errors can become creative opportunities. How will create opportunities from errors or mistakes?

Legacy

On your death bed how will you answer these questions? "Have you made a difference? Is anything different because you were here? Has your life on this planet made the planet any different than it would have been if you hadn't been here? How have you made a difference? Have you put children here that are now leading productive, helpful lives to others (that's one way to make a difference). Have you created business results that have helped people to be employed? Did your business help people to have a better quality of life? Did you serve people that now serve others? What have you done that has made a difference?"

Preparation

Create a morning ritual from the time you awaken in the morning until you arrive at work. Use this time to improve positive attitude, effectiveness, and confidence.

Consider that each and every day, someone, somewhere someone needs your services. Your job is to find them. Where will you seek to find them?

The night before you go back to work ritual is a review of the coming week. Prepare clothes for each day to match weather/events and menu planning. This proactive ritual saves you time and energy helping you to feel and look like a million bucks. Block your time but not too tightly. Give yourself room to breathe, relax, focus so that you can serve more greatly and graciously throughout your day. Use a visualization exercise prior to each encounter with a prospect where you are making the largest impact on the prospect.

Self-Knowledge

Self-awareness is primary to authenticity. To be able to create or author the self you must first understand yourself, and have a desire for ongoing personal growth, and insight. What strengths do you possess that will help you succeed in this business? Why are you enough? Why will you succeed? Why is your age and sex an advantage? What factors will make you succeed? What background experience, skills, and strengths do you personally bring to this business? Write a short paragraph stating your strengths and growing edges. Discuss how you will turn your growing edges into creative opportunities. What obstacles may get in your way? How will you overcome these obstacles? What has helped others to overcome these difficulties? How can reinventing yourself help you capitalize on these challenges?

Public Knowledge

Prospects do not need to know everything about you nor do they need to, however there is some knowledge that you want people to have about you. What do people need to know about you? How will they find this information out? Websites or FB pages are good locations for people to learn about you. Done correctly internet media can be reassuring to prospects. Of course the converse can also be true so consider carefully what you choose to put into the public eye.

Fears

What fears do you have[18]? How will you manage your fears? How will you overcome your negative self-talk? How will you motivate yourself? How will you manage fear?

---

[18] Recommended reading: *Fearless: Creating the Courage to Change the Things You Can*, Steve Chandler (2008)

Self-Care

Your own self-care is paramount to serving your clients with great value. So you well-being is primary to a successful business. How will you ensure that you take care of yourself? What will be your practice for self-care? How will you create positive habits to assist you in your business? How will you create the time to do what you love?

How will you manage "no"? How will you not become discouraged? Be respectful of a "no" but consider that a "no", may be a, "I don't know enough" or a "not yet".

How and what can you learn from the people that really upset you? How will you come to understand others? How will you manage your fear through understanding? How will this serve you?

Internal Management[19]

How will you manage rejection? How can you let go of worrying about what others think of you? How will you not take things personally? How can you use what others say to improve yourself and your business quest? How will you remain flexible and growing throughout this process? How can you become emotionally independent, free of what others think or feel about you? Are you to manage your feelings and emotions as your own? Why or why not?

What will you have to do differently to improve your relationships with others?

---

[19] Recommended Reading: *Loving What Is,* Byron Katie (2003)

How can you serve your clients with a positive attitude and spirit? How can you operate from your highest consciousness in your relationships? If you are the problem. How can that resolve all your problems?

How can you build an inner optimism[20]? How do you talk to yourself? As a friend? How can you talk to yourself as your own best friend?

Where will you have "to act as if"? Until it becomes natural. What is awkward or difficult for you that you need to practice? How will you do that?

---

[20] Recommended reading: *Quest for a Light-Heart*, Marsha Ferrick Heiden (2015)

How can you eliminate criticism from your conversations? How can you create new agreements to establish new behaviors?

How will you live forward given what you have learned and reflected upon about yourself from your past?

How can you improve your focus? Be specific.

How can you be honest and straightforward? Not lying to yourself and to others?

Look inside to find your intention[21]. Find your purpose. What are the differences you want to make? What kind of difference-making makes you feel happy? Then figure out how to do that thing that makes you happy and helps others.

---

[21] Recommended reading: *Quest for Your Life Purpose*, Marsha Ferrick Heiden (2015)

Consider what you don't want[22]. How will you say no to it? How will you know you need to say "no" to it?

Challenge your worst case scenario? What is the worst that can happen? Then ask yourself is it true?

Generating Positivity

My grandmother use to repeat this quote to me, "Act as if everything depended on you. Pray as if everything depended on God."[23] How will you practice trusting that the world is abundant? How will you maintain your faith and trust you've made the right decision going into this business? Consider some of the following exercise: Positive affirmations turned into why questions, "Why am I so prosperous?" Keep a gratitude journal each day. Write down five things you are grateful for each day. A positivity journal of three positive things that happened that day. Create rituals for mornings, evenings, going back to work, returning from work, weekends that keep you

---

[22] Recommended reading: Quest for Boundaries, Marsha Ferrick Heiden (2015)

[23] Saint Ignatius Loyola

and your life running smoothly and efficiently. Formulate a gratitude symbol or create a physical item that reminds you to be grateful throughout your day. Create a play list of upbeat songs, or a list of positive quotes to keep you optimistic and motivated. Consider daily readings and meditation. What might work for you? Which will you try?

Leadership

How can lead yourself and others? How can be someone that others want to follow? How can you create clear agreements with others to avoid the disappoint of expectations[24]?

Practice Saying Your Fees
Where and how can you practice saying your prices and fees? Tape record yourself. Listen to yourself. Keep doing it until you are comfortable with it.

---

[24] Recommended reading: *Straight-Line Leadership: Tools for Living with Velocity and Power in Turbulent Times,* Dusan Djukich

The Challenge of Receptivity

The key to effective giving is to stay open to receiving.[25]

How will you stay open to new opportunities in the environment?

How can you celebrate that which you want more of?

How can you let the love flow out to others in the world so it can make its way back to you?

---

[25] *The Go-Giver* by Bob Burg and John David Mann (2015)

The Holy Grail

It is time to summarize your business. What would you say about your business if you were in a five-minute conversation with an interested individual? What is your business? Who will be served by your business? What future vision do you have for you and your business? Be professional, enthusiastic, and concise.

For additional books or information visit

www.amaraquest.com

www.ingramcontent.com/pod-product-compliance
Lightning Source LLC
Chambersburg PA
CBHW052051190326
41519CB00002BA/188